Shuts & Passages of Shrewsbury

BY

A. SCOTT-DAVIES & R. S. SEARS

SHROPSHIRE LIBRARIES
1986

Revised Edition 1989
  Shuts and passages of Shrewsbury.
  1. Shrewsbury (Shropshire)—Description
  —Guide-books
  I. Title II. Sears, R.S.
  914.24'54 DA690.S58
  ISBN 0903802341
  Cover Illustration by A. Scott-Davies.
  Cover Design and Realization: Les Walton.
  Published by Shropshire Libraries, London Road, Shrewsbury.
  Printed by Redverse Ltd., Shrewsbury.
  © A. Scott-Davies.

CONTENTS

INTRODUCTION

Shrewsbury must be more fortunate than other towns in the number and nature of the shuts and passages that have survived the ravages of time and town planner alike. At first sight they may seem of little consequence, but having lived in Shrewsbury, you begin to appreciate them enormously. They provide excellent short cuts from one point to another and are pleasant backwaters, free from the hustle and bustle of the main streets. It is possible by judicious selection of route to travel right round the centre without hardly walking down a main street. In addition, they often give the pedestrian glimpses of the town that would otherwise be hidden behind the modern shop facades.

The word "shut" is unusual in that it seems to imply a closed alleyway or thoroughfare. Its origin is rather obscure, although it has been suggested that it may derive from the "Schutte" family, who once owned a house in Drayton's Passage. They almost certainly gave their name to "Shoplatch", an adjoining street recorded in 1295 as "Scheteplache". Whatever the origin of the word, it was not unique to Shrewsbury. The "Shropshire Word Book" (1879) by Miss Georgina Jackson mentions the existence of shuts in Wellington, Ellesmere and Oswestry. Miss Jackson also quotes from Rev. J. B. Blakeway's work on the history of Salop as follows:

> *"From the stalls or Mardol-Head the street itself of Mardol branches off to the right, but the straightforward course which we are now pursuing brings us into the narrow street called Shoplatch: at the entrance to which is the passage of Gullet Shut. A shut in Shrewsbury language denotes, not, as might be imagined, a cul-de-sac or alley shut at one end, but, on the contrary, one open at both extremities, enabling the pedestrian, for it is previous only to such, to shoot or*

move rapidly from one street into another."
Blakeway, Salop, M.S.S. (a.d. 1817).

No doubt debate about the origins of the word will continue, as will research into the shuts and passages that survive, as well as the ones that are lost. Their names conjure up wonderful pictures of a Dickensian world: Factory Shut, Sheep's Head Shut, Turkey Shut, Leopard Shut and Spoon Passage. These are just a few of the ones that have disappeared; the town must indeed have been a veritable rabbit warren. I suppose we should be thankful that we have so many left. I hope you will enjoy exploring them and perhaps you too will come to appreciate the special character they give our much loved town.

Author's Note to the Revised Edition
Since Shuts and Passages of Shrewsbury was published in 1986 Owen's Passage, Bythell's Passage and Seventy Steps Shut have been demolished during the redevelopment of Pride Hill.

The greatest loss to the town has to be Seventy Steps Shut removed to make way for a concrete stairway into the new Darwin Shopping Centre.

Let us hope the other 21 shuts can withstand the onslaught of progress.

March 1989

iv

GULLET PASSAGE

Possibly took its name from the Gullet Inn that stood along its route, although the reverse could be true. The Inn is believed to have been owned by a certain Molly Miles. An old Shrewsbury ditty mentioning both is quoted by Georgina Jackson in her "Shropshire Word Book" of 1879:–

> *"Don't you know the muffin man,*
> *Don't you know his name,*
> *Don't you know the muffin man,*
> *That lives in our lane?*
> *All round the Butter-Cross,*
> *Up and down St. Giles's,*
> *Up and down the Gullet Shut,*
> *And call at Molly Miles's."*
>
> Old Shrewsbury ditty.

Part of the Gullet Inn is now a public house called "The Hole in the Wall", the rest making up small shops along the passage.

As far back as the Middle Ages, there was a stream which ran down Gullet Passage to a place called Mudholes (near the Welsh Bridge). The Square, which the passage joins, was once a pool or bog feeding the stream. With the Middle English for stream being "Golate", this could be an alternative origin of the name "Gullet". The remains of gate hinges and bolt holes in the entrance to The Square could give support to the theory that "shut" derives from the Medieval practice of closing the passages after dark.

Gullet Passage

Directions:

From the Tourist Information Centre, cross the road to the left of the Magistrates' Court heading towards the Williams and Glyn Bank. Gullet Passage is found along the side of the bank, nearest to the Information Centre.

PLOUGH SHUT

The Plough Shut originally went from the Square to Mardol Head under the Plough Inn, although now because of modernisation the shut is a dead end. It was known as the Throughway until 1890 when the 16th Century timber-framed building underwent a major restoration with a third storey being added. The three gables have enriched barge boards crowning the six transomed, mullioned, bay windows set on corbel brackets. The box frame has a fine array of cable mouldings with the upper floor enriched with ornamental framing, the best view of which is from the Square and not the shut.

It would appear from records that its use as an Inn is a recent one with a mention, in 1672, as the Selds or Shields (SELDA=M.E., shop or stall) this was an area renowned for its drapers, so much so that the Square was often called 'The Drapery'.

Plough Shut

Directions:

Having walked through Gullet Passage turn right up Shoplatch. Between the NatWest Bank and Millets you will find Plough Shut.

GROPE LANE

An early name for this passage is recorded as 'Grope Counte Lane' (1324) when it was a dark and narrow passage through which one groped one's way. It has also been known as Gropelone and Le Grope Lane. Sir Richard Stury, together with Sir Richard Acton, took up residence here in the 15th Century.

At the bottom of Grope Lane (High Street, left) stands Dormie Outfitters in a building of the 16th Century, of timber frame and plaster, formerly the 'Cross Keys Inn'. The Inn was called 'The Globe' from 1780 until it became the 'Cross Keys' in 1820 when the Inn opposite, also the 'Cross Keys' was demolished to make way for the Shirehall (now also demolished). The Mercer's Company, who were a group of Shrewsbury merchants, held many of their meetings here for years. The building became a shop soon after 1911 when it was delicensed.

Despite a few modern touches in the shop facades, it is fair to say that this lane retains much of its former atmosphere. Although with modern sanitation and lack of animals in the town, what atmosphere it does retain does not include the smells. As well as a feel for old Shrewsbury, it also provides an excellent route from High Street to Fish Street and the Bear Steps.

Grope Lane

Directions:

From the entrance of the Plough Shut, carry on up Shoplatch, crossing the road opposite Owen Owen. Here look across the road to see Ireland's Mansion, an outstanding black and white residence built in 1575. Carry on up High Street where, on the left between a shoe shop and Dormie Outfitters, one can find Grope Lane.

BEAR STEPS

So called because the 'Bear Inn' stood at its entrance in Fish Street (a reference to the fish markets held in the street) from 1780-1910. The steps go under a timber-framed arch, part of a complex of small buildings which were restored in 1976 by the Shrewsbury Civic Society, who now have their office over the small coffee house (right). The restoration received a heritage year award on its completion for its principal feature of a medieval hall, now used for exhibitions and meetings.

Bear Steps

Directions:

Almost opposite the exit of Grope Lane can be found the entrance to the shortest of the passages, Bear Steps.

SAINT ALKMUND'S PASSAGE

In the Square of St. Alkmund's stands St. Julian's House, a fine Victorian pastiche of a timber-framed building, built with natural wood, transomed, mullioned, leaded, bay windows. A lively style of pattern with richly coloured and carved panels above the door forming an impressive portal. The Square was once called Old Fish Street, it later became Berrington Square, named after the Berrington family who resided nearby, finally because of the Shrewsbury Street Act of 1825 it became St. Alkmund's Square.

The church of St. Alkmund's (opposite) was founded in 912 A.D., having a very fine stained glass window signed by Francis Egington, 1795, a copy of Guido Reni's *'Assumption'* that is well worth a visit.

Saint Alkmund's Passage

Directions:

Having ascended the Bear Steps, turn right following the church wall. Turn left up Church Street, passing the Prince Rupert Pizza Bar. Upon reaching St. Mary's Street, turn right into Dogpole. After some 50 yards St. Alkmund's Passage can be seen on your right.

8

ST. JULIAN'S SHUT

Leading to the east of the old St. Julian's Church, now an established craft centre, this shut joins Wyle Cop at one end and St. Alkmund's Square and Passage at the other.

Along its route one passes a fascinating stone coffin carved in the shape of a person complete with a drain hole at the lower end. These were very popular for many centuries. This one was discovered during restoration work in the Victorian period.

The foundations of the church are Saxon and the tower which now serves as living accommodation is 12th to 15th century.

Halfway along the shut is the entrance to St. Julian's Place, a well-tended garden now open to the public with benches for the weary to sit and rest.

St. Julian's Shut

Directions:

From St. Alkmund's Passage progress towards St. Alkmund's Church. Turn left toward St. Julian's Craft Centre. Follow the shut before descending steps into Wyle Cop.

BANK PASSAGE

At the Fish Street entrance to Bank Passage stands, on the right, Wesley House, an early 18th Century house with a simple door case and stucco to upper storey. The plaque on its wall reads "JOHN WESLEY PREACHED HERE 1761".

The passage was once called Twenty Steps Shut but has since lost four of these, there being only 16 steps in this partly cobbled passage. The High Street end has, on the right, the remains of a Victorian facade erected to give the Bank's side entrance an affluent appearance, the Bank standing on this site until 1910. Stone foundations to be found just in from the facade may well be those of the house owned by Sir John Burgh, a notable personage in the reign of Edward IV and five times Sheriff of Shropshire.

The loss of four steps (if indeed there were 20) may be due to the general renovation of the passage in 1846. A plaque commemorating this is to be seen above the door at the bottom of the steps. It reads:

> "These steps were gratuitously renewed by C. M. Adams Esq., and Mr. Richard Davies, at their joint expense, for the benefit of the public in August 1846."

I can only assume that Mr. Adams and Mr. Davies were extremely modest men because the plaque is easily missed and when found, difficult to read.

Bank Passage

Directions:

Almost opposite the exit of St. Alkmund's Passage is the entrance to St. Alkmund's churchyard. Follow the path to the left of the church, descend the steps (the church is well worth a visit). Turn left at the bottom of the steps down Fish Street. Bank Passage is to be found on your right to the left of Wesley House.

12

BARRACKS PASSAGE

Also known as Elisha's Shut after the family who lived in a house at the Wyle Cop entrance. Samuel Elisha served as Mayor in 1725, his son Edward became Mayor in 1743.

Barracks Passage is said to have been given its name because soldiers were billeted in the timber-framed building on the left, now in a state of decay. Standing in front of the Wyle Cop entrance, look up and to your left at the Henry Tudor House, where there is a plaque reading:

> "YE ANCIENT HOUSE IN WHICH KING HENRY 7th
> LODGED WHEN HE WENT TO BOSWORTH FIELD
> AUG. 1485".

This was the battle in which Richard III was killed and Henry was proclaimed King Henry VII, so ending the War of the Roses, founding the Tudor Dynasty.

The Lion Hotel at one time had a tap room to the left of the passage and hence it was, for a short time, referred to as Lion Tap Passage.

Barracks Passage

Directions:

Leaving Bank Passage turn left, walking along High Street. Cross to Wyle Cop opposite St. Julian's Craft Centre. Turn left down the Cop, passing the Lion Hotel. Barracks Passage is next to the first black and white building on the right.

14

COMPASSES PASSAGE

In 1878, No. 71 Wyle Cop was the Compasses Inn, a timber-framed building showing examples of carpenters' marks which were used away from the site of erection by the carpenters, who would cut into the upper face of joining timbers, a code for erection from the prefabricated state of the house. Four yards in from the Wyle Cop, on the right, is a fine example of a moulded wooden door case dating to the 1750s, which at some time has been damaged. Carry on to Belmont Bank. Again, on your right, you can see the decaying timber-framed buildings of Barracks Passage.

Leaving the passage, turn down the Wyle Cop where, two doors down is Bowdler's Passage, which unfortunately is a private passage although its use as a public passage seems to go back to the 1700s, before Bowdler's School was built.

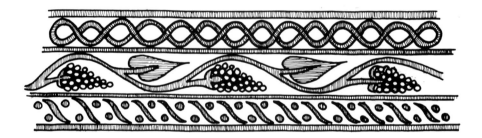

Compasses Passage

Directions:

Leaving Barracks Passage, turn left and follow Belmont Bank down approximately 25 yards, where you will come across Compasses Passage. This looks like a private alley, but is not. Leaving the passage, turn right. Two shops down you will notice another passage, known as Bowdler's Passage. This unfortunately is a private passage, although its use as a public passage seems to go back to the 1700s, when Bowdler's School was built.

GOLDEN CROSS PASSAGE

Golden Cross Passage was previously known as Sextry Shut, derived from the proximity of the sacristry belonging to St. Chad's Church. It stood at the Princess Street end, connected to the church by means of a covered elevated walkway, which appears to be have been removed in 1794.

It was later known as Steel Yard Shut, taken from the medieval slang word 'Stilliard', meaning 'a place in which foreign people, especially German, met to trade in goods'. It kept this name until 1795 when it changed to Golden Cross Passage, named after the Inn to be found within the passage. The Inn is the oldest existing in the town and one of the oldest in the country, dating to 1495. During the Civil War it became a meeting place for prominent Shrewsbury Royalists, including Sir Michael Ernley, Sir Francis Ottley and Sir Richard Lee.

Golden Cross Passage

Directions:

Leaving Bowdler's Passage, head back up the Wyle Cop then turn left into Milk Street. Before turning right into Princess Street, look up at the end elevation of the old St. Chad's. The inscription is as follows:

> "In this sacred enclosure stood the ancient church of St. Chad's which was founded A.D.DCCLXXX. The first Saxon church in Shrewsbury. Collegiate, spacious and cruciform was erected on the same site A.D.MCCCXCIII. It fell July 1, X.M.DCCLXXXVII. This usually called the Bishop's chancel being the only extant."

17

PEACOCK PASSAGE

Was named after the Inn which stood at the High Street end of the passage between 1780-1820. At the other end stood the timber-framed King's Head, which also gave its name to the shut between 1643-1780, and as with the Peacock, it closed its doors in 1920 when it became a shop until its demolition in 1937. The passage is arched at both ends, the High Street entrance having an unusual wooden surround of black and gold.

Peacock Passage

Directions:

At the end of Golden Cross Passage, turn left down the High Street, or "Gumblestolestrete" as it was known in medieval times. Keep going until you are opposite the entrance of Bank Passage, where you will find Peacock Passage.

COFFEE HOUSE PASSAGE

The passage was named after an 18th Century house of entertainment which stood at its entrance in the Square. Just inside the passage, if you look upwards to the ceiling, you will see a carved beam with '1577 G.P.' bordered by a grape and vine motif. Beyond this at the end of the covered section, looking up at the side of the Coffee House, a plaque can be seen with just three letters as follows: B
      R A

These may well be the owner's initials, which often appear on buildings in the town.

Coffee House Passage

Directions:

From Peacock Passage turn right and follow Princess Street into the Square. Stay on the left path, passing H. Lee and Son's grocery shop, after which is Coffee House Passage.

DRAYTON'S PASSAGE

Also known as Eddowes's Shut because it led to the works of Eddowes Printers. When they left in 1750 the passage changed to Drayton's Passage and was known as such in 1880.

During the recent restoration of much of the passage, the lower floors of a building were uncovered, possibly dating from 1325-1350. A house in the passage was owned by the Shete or Shutte family, who gave their name to Shoplatch (Shutte-Place) and may well have been the origin of the word 'Shut'.

It is said that the passage carried straight on, through to the Square, going under the house directly in front, with applications being made to Alderman Hughes, the owner, for the passage to keep its course through his wine cellars!

Drayton's Passage

Directions:

Turn right out of Coffee House Passage and head down College Hill. Turn right down Swan Hill. Another right will take you into Market Street and opposite our last passage of this section, Drayton's Passage. Once through the passage, turn right, right again, walking up Gullet Passage to the Square.

21

BYTHELL'S PASSAGE

Bythell's Passage was named after a chemist who, for many years, occupied the shop standing at its entrance in Pride Hill, now Jean Jeanies. Its original course was to the Raven Meadows, but this was altered when a garage was built, cutting the passage in half and, as with Drayton's Passage, it is diverted by a sudden right angle. At the time of writing the area around and behind this passage is due to be redeveloped and it may soon disappear.

Bythell's Passage

Directions:

From the Tourist Information Centre, walk again to the left of the Magistrates' Court, but instead of going down Gullet Passage walk towards the Clive Monument. Cross the road and head off up Pride Hill pedestrian area. On your left is Jean Jeanie and to the right of the shop is Bythell's Passage.

DICKEN'S COURT

This court is one of three newly created passages, the others being incorporated in Mardol Gardens and the Victorian Arcade. Dicken's Court was named in 1982 when the Victorian Arcade was opened to the public. It is partly cobbled, with a large iron gate which is closed between the hours of 6 p.m. and 8 a.m. Before the development of this whole area, there were several shuts with interesting names such as Factory Shut, Turkey Shut and Spoon Passage, the latter so named because of a large wooden spoon that hung above a spoon maker's shop.

Dicken's Court

Directions:

From Bythell's Passage head down Pride Hill to Lloyds Bank. Turn right down Roushill Bank and left at its junction with Roushill. Passing the telephone boxes, make your way to the Raven Wine Bar, opposite which is Hill's Lane. Dicken's Court is just off Hill's Lane about 50 yards down to your right.

VICTORIAN ARCADE

Dicken's Court joins up with the Victorian Arcade, which also has entrances off Hill's Lane and Mardol. This is a shopping arcade of modern origins (1982), but with a Victorian theme. The thoroughfares are covered and small, creating a cosy, intimate atmosphere. The shops sell all manner of things from antiques to photographic film. On a hot day the arcade provides a cool arbour and in the winter months a welcome respite from the elements.

The majority of the site was formerly occupied by a cigarette factory, the only other known link between Hill's Lane and Mardol being Carnarvon Lane. So it would seem even modern development can create shuts of a sort.

Victorian Arcade

Directions:

Dicken's Court joins up with the Victorian Arcade, which is an attempt to create a Victorian street complex which works well. Turn left out of the arcade to reach Hill's Lane once again.

24

CARNARVON LANE

Carnarvon Lane is one of the few to keep its name since inception and is thought to have been named as a reminder of the trade links with the north coast of Wales. Conway and Bangor also have streets or houses named after them. In 1460, however, a Ludovick Carnarvon resided at the Hill's Lane entrance of the passage and offers a more feasible reason for the name. At the other end, as late as 1905, stood a confectioner's shop owned by Mrs. Hillier, with Davies, Ebenezer Co., who were hardware dealers, in the shop opposite.

Carnarvon Lane

Directions:

Carnarvon Lane is one of the few to keep its name since inception. From the Hill's Lane entrance to the Victorian Arcade, turn right towards the Queen Victoria pub; at the corner of this Carnarvon Lane stands, leading through to the Mardol.

26

KING'S HEAD PASSAGE

King's Head Passage follows the side of the King's Head Inn to the Smithfield Road. This is not to be confused with the King's Head Shut, which was situated in Princess Street, now called Peacock Passage. The remains of a stone tower, believed to be those of a guard tower belonging to the town wall of 1150, existed on the left until quite recently. Little now remains. The passage dates to 1674.

King's Head Inn is an unusually attractive timber-frame and plaster building characteristic of the late 15th Century. Having three storeys gives away the fact that it was heavily restored in the early 19th Century. There are two six-light, moulded wood, mullioned windows with Gothic traceried heads. It was previously known as the 'Last Inn' until the early 1800s, when the original King's Head was transferred lower down the street to its present position. A fine tile border in the entrance to the inn dates to the 14th Century and was probably made in Broseley, Shropshire, with their impressed pattern filled with a yellow slip to give a vivid contrast to the red of the ground.

King's Head Passage

Directions:

From Carnarvon Lane, cross the road. Now walk a few yards up and between the Army Careers Centre and the King's Head pub, where you will find the King's Head Passage.

28

PHOENIX PLACE

Phoenix Place was previously called Mason's Shut and Shackleton's Shut, its earliest recorded name. The present passage is named after Mr. Phoenix, who kept a baker's shop at No. 53 The Mardol, a fine example of a timber-framed building showing an overhang which was a way of increasing floor space on the upper floors. A little further down, under the first arch, just after the cobbled pathway, untreated timbers exist in an almost original state, for it was not until the 19th Century that timbers were painted in the now familiar black and white. Often they were whitewashed with lime to protect the buildings against the rain.

Further down the passage can be seen the bricked-up windows and doors of some former houses. In their book on "Victorian Shrewsbury", the Victorian Shrewsbury Research Group point out the unusual nature of the occupants' livelihood in a chapter headed "Red Light in Roushill". Joyce Butt, the author of that particular chapter, has studied extensively the census of 1861, as well as the newspapers of the day. Her efforts were aided by the enumerator of the 1861 census, who conscientiously recorded all brothels and prostitutes as such. It turns out that the whole Roushill area was the centre of Victorian Shrewsbury's red light district. It seems a far cry from the quiet backwater of the present day.

Phoenix Place

Directions:

Turn right out of the King's Head Passage along Smithfield Road. Walk around the corner past the Proud Salopian pub. Continue to walk towards Roushill Bank and after you pass an ironmonger's you will come across Phoenix Place, which has the appearance of a car parking area.

MARDOL GARDENS

Mardol Gardens, like the Victorian Arcade, was built in 1982, but unlike the arcade it has no overall theme. It provides a route from Mardol through to Roushill, which is partly covered and lined with shops. One larger area is given over to an indoor market and the whole makes for a pleasant stroll, free as it is from traffic.

The exit into Roushill is opposite the Riverside Shopping Centre, a modern complex which stands on the site of the old livestock market. Called The Smithfield, it stood here from 1850 up until the late 1950s, when it was transferred to a site on the outskirts of town. It must in its time have enlivened the whole Mardol area, bringing much welcome trade on market days. The recent development of the Victorian Arcade and Mardol Gardens will hopefully contribute in a similar way to the revival of present day businesses in the area.

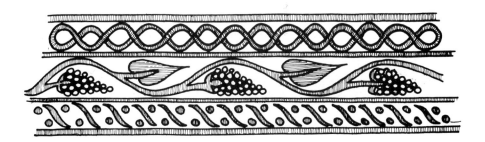

Mardol Gardens

Directions:

Turn left out of Phoenix Place towards the Cinema, after which is a shop and Mardol Gardens, which has become a second arcade for small shops although it takes on the appearance of a modern indoor market. Right through the Mardol Gardens will bring you out into Roushill and the Riverside Shopping Centre.

SEVENTY STEPS SHUT

This shut was also known as Burley's Shut, the name of a painter who had his workshop at the bottom of the steps in 1730. Later to be known as Waggon and Horses Shut, taken from the name of the Inn which stood on the site of Dunn and Co. The Inn was previously known as the Plume of Feathers from 1786 until 1804, when it became the Plume and Feathers before its change to the Waggon and Horses between 1828 and 1883, when it was owned by the Trent Valley Motor Company. It was once called a "Disorderly House".

At the time of writing, the area around and behind Seventy Steps Shut is due to be redeveloped. The steps, as they are at the moment, may soon disappear.

Seventy Steps Shut

Directions:

From Mardol Gardens and Roushill, walk towards the footbridge and the multi-storey car park. Before you reach the Park Lane Nightclub, a rough car park is situated on the right. The Seventy Steps Shut runs from the left-hand corner of here along the side of an old slaughter house.

OWEN'S PASSAGE

The original Owen's Passage went down the side of the Raven, a hotel now demolished to make way for Woolworth's. The present passage goes along the side of Woolworth's, connecting Castle Street with the Riverside Shopping Centre and car park via a footbridge.

The Raven, which stood to the left of Owen's Passage, was one of the principal Inns of the town for at least 250 years and occupied the site of Thorne's Hall, which had been moved to the other side of the street. Sir Vincent Corbett seems to have bought the Raven from the Thorne family in 1686 and this could be the reason for its name, as the Corbett family badge is the Raven.

In 1705 the dramatist George Farquhar is said to have written his comedy "The Recruiting Officer" here. Later he dedicated it to "All Friends Round The Wrekin". In 1753 there was held the first meeting of the Shrewsbury Hunt, and by the late 1750s the Raven became the principal coaching Inn until the Lion Hotel gained prominence in 1779. Robert Lawrence operated the first post coach from the Raven to Holyhead. Its gardens were said to be in excess of 3 acres, which were evidently in the area occupied now by the car park and Telecom House.

At the time of writing, the whole of the passage is usable, although it must be said that the whole of its course is of modern origin. The ground underfoot is concrete, as are the parapet walls that run along the elevated section to the back of Woolworth's, the view from which is the only thing worth mentioning.

Directions:

From the top of the Seventy Steps Shut, turn left up Pride Hill towards the monument to Hotspur and David Prince of Wales, who were hung, drawn and quartered on the spot after Henry IV's victory in the Battle of Shrewsbury. Pass Marks and Spencer, Littlewoods and Woolworth's. The original Owen's Passage ran along the side of the Raven, a hotel demolished to make way for Woolworth's. The new passage is to the right of Woolworth's.

CASTLE COURT

Castle Court used to be called House of Correction Shut, where the old prison stood with its marvellous nail-studded door now giving entrance to the Old Police House Restaurant.

The defunct church to the left is at present the Multiskills Youth Centre. It was built in 1826 for the Primitive Methodists and has, or had, no name as such. It was still in use as a place of worship up until 1956 when, for whatever reason, the congregation moved to the church on St. John's Hill. As W. E. Morris puts it in his history of Methodism in Shrewsbury and District, "The fellowship of the church was enriched and strengthened by the reception of members formerly of Castle Court Church".

Castle Court

Directions:

From Woolworth's (Owen's Passage), carry on down Castle Street towards the Castle until, on your left, is seen Castle Court and the Old Police House Restaurant.

SAINT MARY'S SHUT

This shut seems rather unpromising at first sight from Castle Street, but the exit into St. Mary's Place is quite charming. In 1805 it was known as the Little Shut, perhaps due to the fact that it was so narrow. The raised covered walkway which goes through the half-timbered house is part of the original route and is still a right of way. It has been restored and the 16th Century building converted into a pair of cottages.

Although it is difficult to know the age of the shut, the church presents even more puzzles; a 13th Century porch, 14th Century chapel, 19th Century chancel east window. The interior is well worth a visit and the 14th Century Jesse window is without doubt the most impressive in the county.

Saint Mary's Shut

Directions:

Cross the road opposite Castle Court, turning right up Castle Street. After crossing the small St. Mary's Street you will reach the last of the town's central shuts. St. Mary's Shut runs along the side of Sidoli's cafe into St. Mary's Place.

GLOSSARY OF TERMS USED FOR THE TIMBER-FRAMED BUILDINGS

Cable Mouldings – These are carved features, usually upright, that have the appearance of rope. The expense involved in incorporating such decorative details must reflect the relevant affluence of the owner/builder.

Corbel Brackets – These are the lengths of timber which project beyond the lower wall of a building, creating an overhang and supporting the upper floors/walls which rest upon them.

Gothic Traceried Heads – These are interlaced carved tops to the mullions in windows to give the Gothic appearance, a practice very fashionable in the 16th Century. One of the best examples in Shrewsbury can be seen at the Henry Tudor House, Wyle Cop, uncovered in 1889.

Overhang – This is where upper floors literally overhang the lower floors. It makes buildings look as though they are leaning into the street. It was used as a way of increasing floor space in the upper storeys and of counterbalancing the tensions set up in a large timber-framed house. The claustrophobic effect it can create in narrow streets is best displayed in Grope Lane.

Quatrefoils – A circle containing four cusps creating a folliated appearance, the number of cusps giving rise to the name, hence: a trefoil, quatrefoil, cinquefoil and multifoil. Quite commonly found in window tracery and ornamental framing.

Stucco – This is white painted plaster which infills the gaps left by the wooden frame of half-timbered buildings. It is supported by either stone slabs, oak laths or wattle, the most common of which is made up of upright hazel or cleft oak, which are woven basket fashion.

Timber-frame and Plaster – Shrewsbury boasts many different styles. Three of the commonest are: (1) The Box or Square Frame in which the wooden frame creates a 'Box' pattern on the surface of the wall; (2) the more decorative 15th/16th Century Ornamental Framing, which uses the Box Frame as a base, but creates lively visual patterns on the wall surface; (3) Close Studding, which as its name suggests, has all upright studs close together.

Transomed and Mullioned – Mullions are the upright posts found in windows. These were the original window's slats, the bad weather being kept out by the use of internal shutters. The later transoms were used to help divide the window space up so that leaded glass panels could be supported.

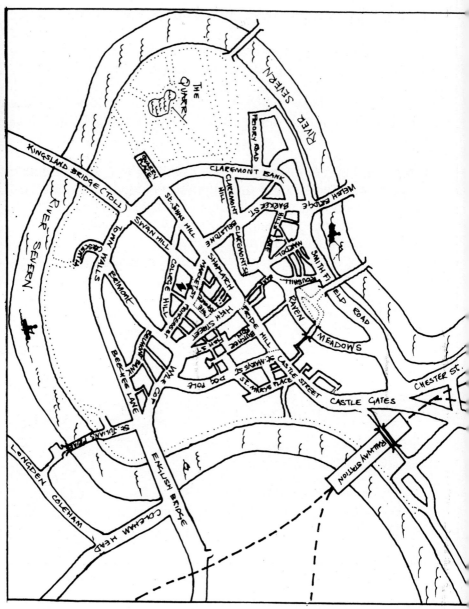

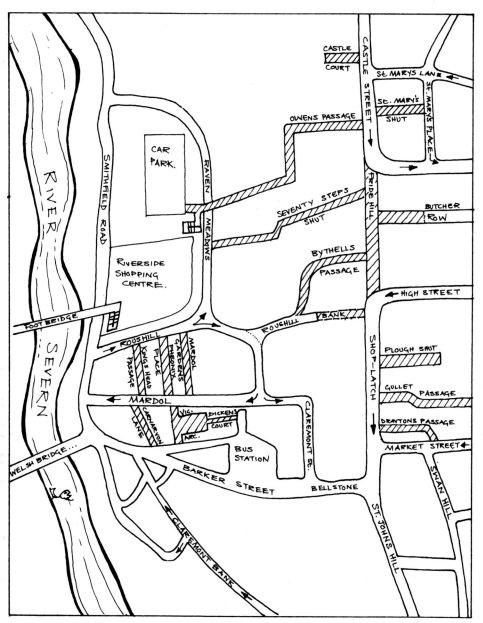

NORTH-WEST AREA OF TOWN CENTRE SHOWING SHUTS AND PASSAGES

KEY: ▨ SHUT, PASSAGE OR PEDESTRIAN AREA

➤ ONE-WAY SYSTEM

41

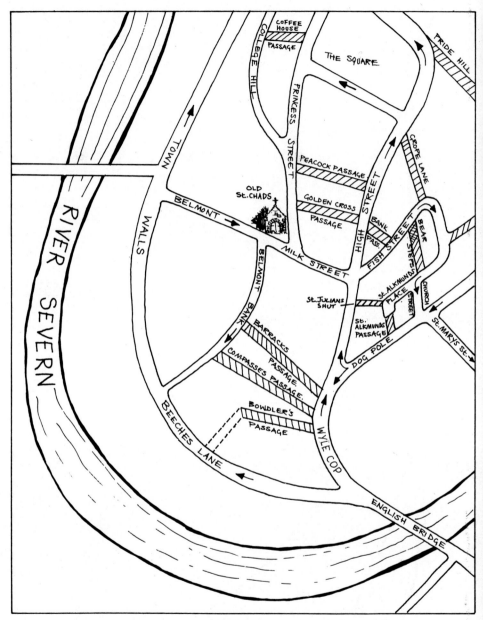

SOUTH-WEST AREA OF TOWN CENTRE SHOWING SHUTS AND PASSAGES

KEY: ▨ SHUT, PASSAGE OR PEDESTRIAN AREA

➜ ONE-WAY SYSTEM

42